ABC
Writing Lesson

Handwriting skills for young children

A practice book
with plenty of pages

Mountcastle

Mountcastle Company
www.readinglesson.com
Email: support@readinglesson.com

Print ISBN 978-0-913063-34-7
Library of Congress Catalog Card Number 99-64110

Art work by: Barbara Zeiring
Book design by: Stephen John Tierney

Printed in the United States, April 2021

The ABC's

The *ABC Writing Lesson* is your child's first step to handwriting.

By now, your child can hold a pencil and draw short straight lines, triangles, squares, and circles. Great! It's time to learn letters. After writing letters becomes automatic, your child will be combining them effortlessly into words. Next, she will be writing words as they pop into her mind, not thinking about the individual letters. She will focus on the content and not on the hand movement.

Handwriting and reading go together. Developing handwriting skills will speed up learning to read. The *ABC Writing Lesson* follows the alphabet and provides practice pages for lower and uppercase letters, and numbers.

Have your child use a soft lead pencil, perhaps with a pencil grip. Remind her not to hold the pencil too tightly and not to press it too hard on the page. For younger children with less developed fine motor control, consider a crayon; using a regular pencil or pen might be too difficult. You will find the upper and lowercase letters are similar in size. At this point only the shape is important; understanding of scale comes later.

Ask your child to trace the letters and copy them in the blank areas with lines. Encourage your child to stay within the lines when tracing letters but not be too strict about how she forms them. Only practice and repetition matter at this point. Every child has a unique writing style and follows their own path of motor development. Be patient, and practice will work its magic.

There is a dotted line around the main picture, have your child trace it. The dotted pictures are also for the child to trace and color for better fine motor control.

If you need additional practice pages, go to the expanded version of this book in printable PDF format on our website, www.readinglesson.com. When ready, move on to the *Teach Me Handwriting* book in this series.

Happy writing from the Giggle Bunny and the Reading Lesson team.

a A

a a a a a

A A A A

a a a a

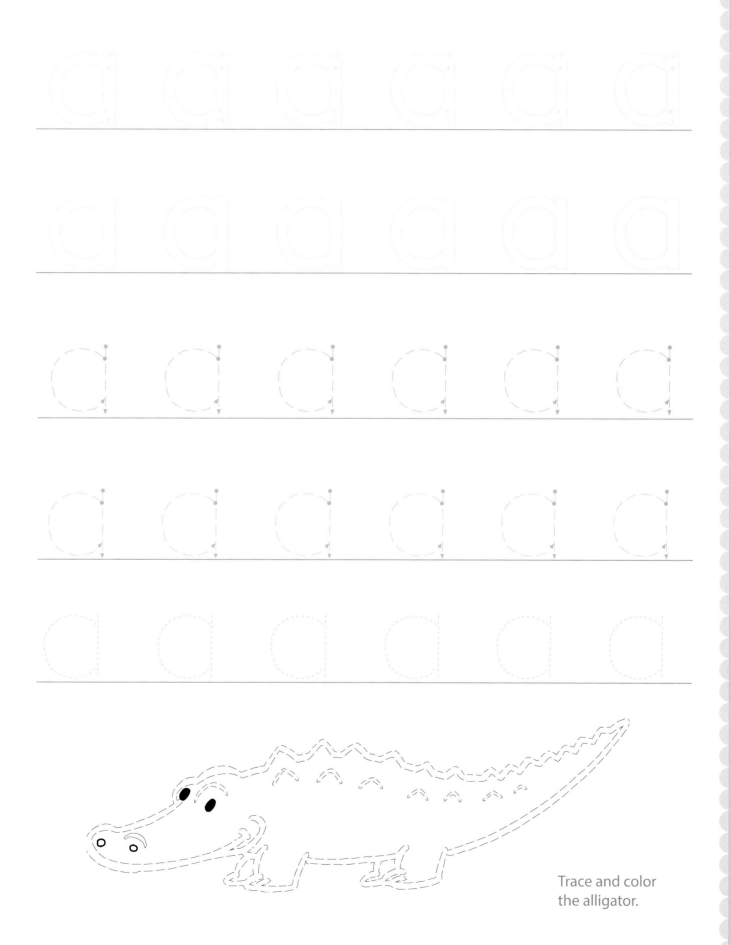

Trace and color
the alligator.

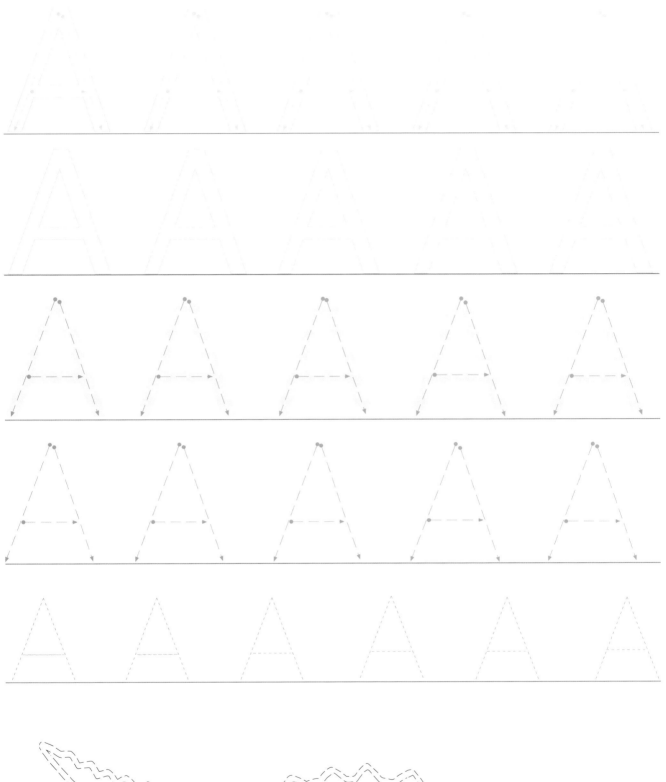

Trace and color
the alligator.

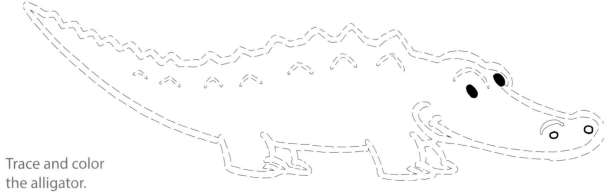

a a a a a a

A A A A A A

a

A

a

A

a

A

a

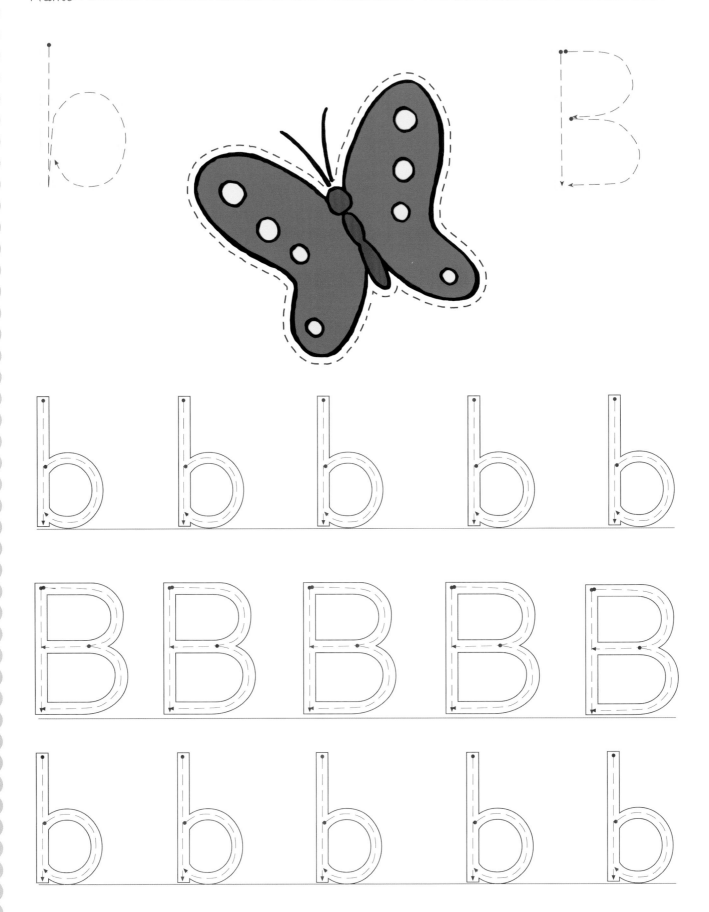

b b b b b b

b b b b b b

b b b b b b

b b b b b b

b b b b b b

b b b

Trace and color
the butterfly.

B B B B B

B B B B

B B B B B

B B B B B

B B B B

B B B

Trace and color
the butterfly.

b b b b b b

B B B B B B

b

B

b

B

b

B

b

Name

C C C C C C

C C C C C C

C C C C C C

C C C C C C

C C C

C C C

Name

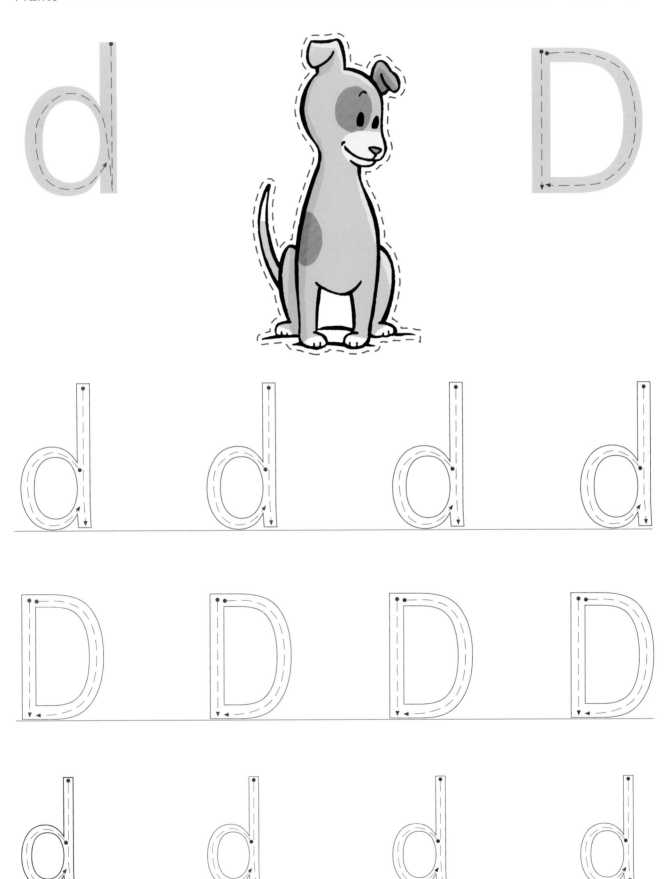

D D D D D D D

D D D D D D

D D D D D D

D D D

D D D

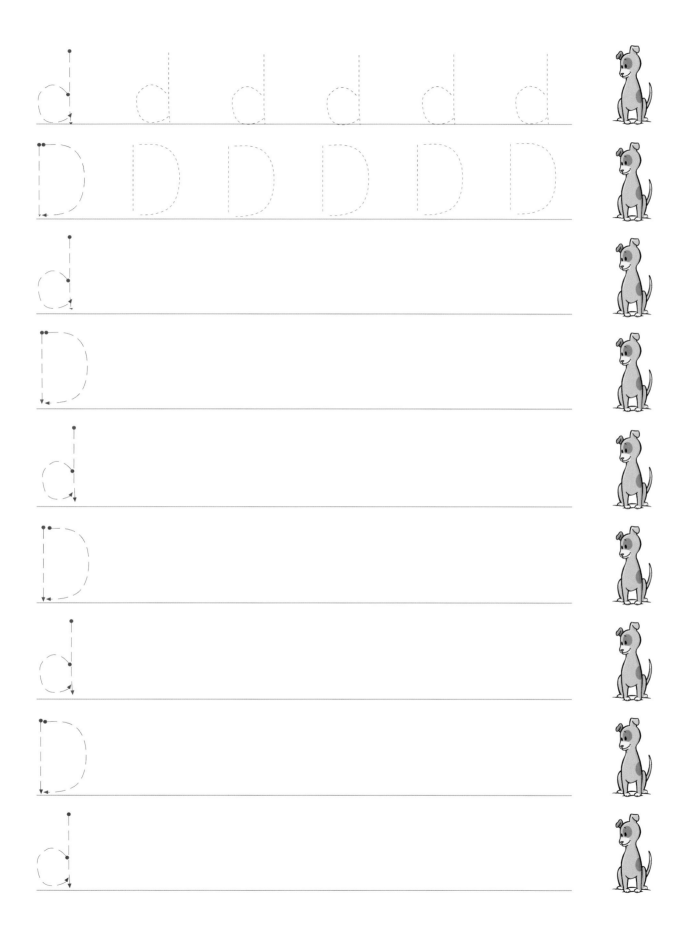

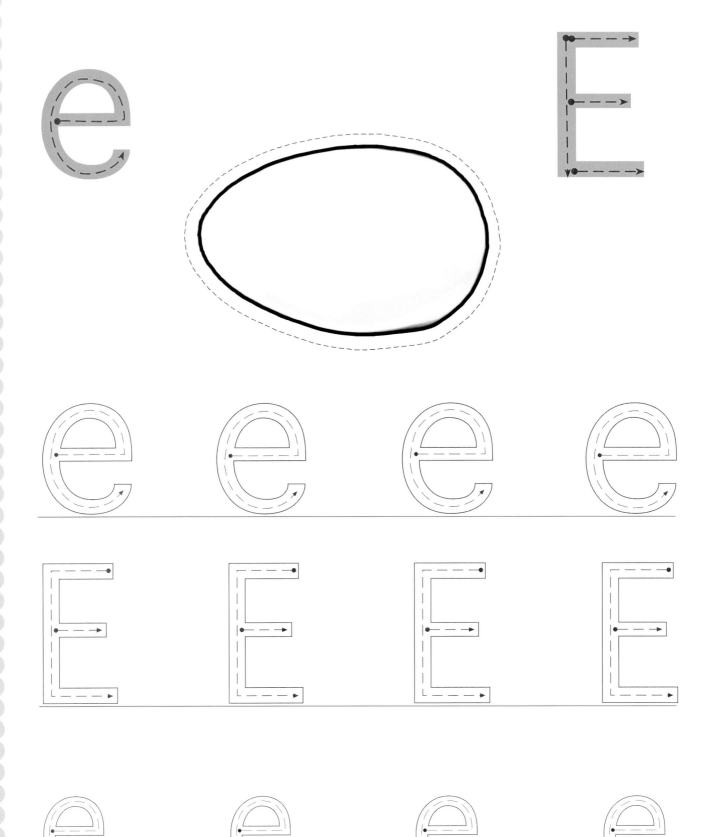

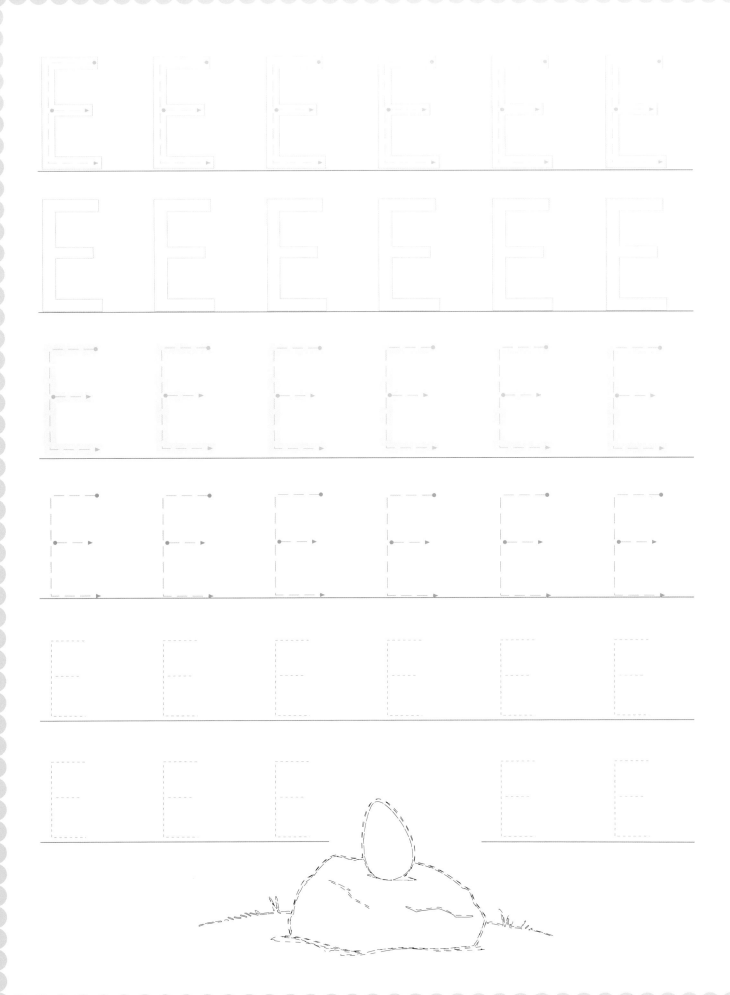

Name _____

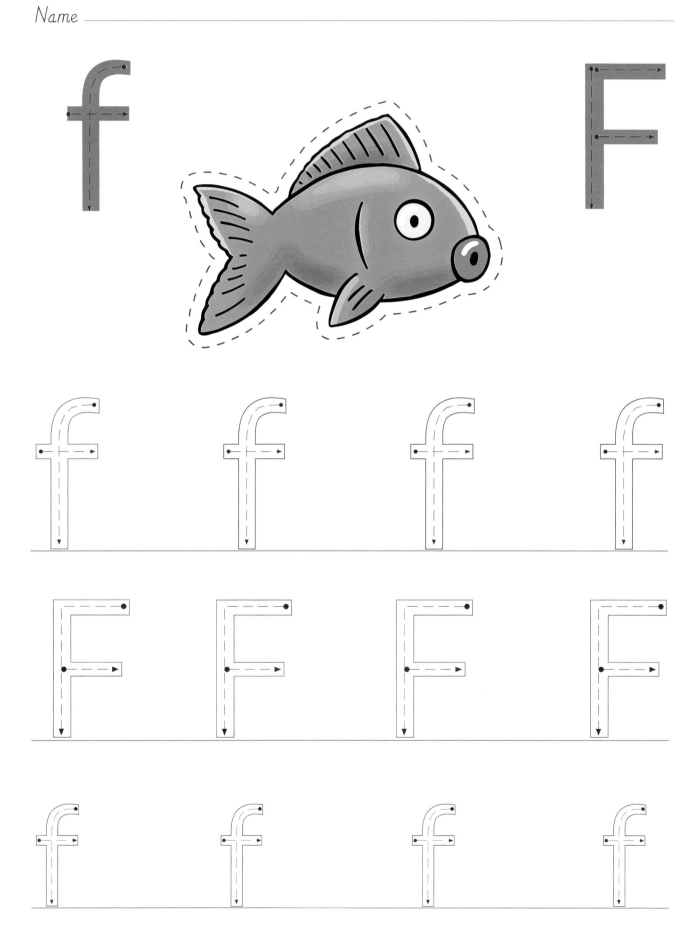

f f f f f f

f f f f f f

f f f f f f

f f f

g  G

g g g g

G G G

g g g g

g g g g g

a g g g g

g g g g g

a a g a g a

g g g g

a a g a

G G G G G G

G G G G G

G G G G G G

G G G G G G

G G G

G G G

g g g g g g

G G G G G G

g

G

g

G

g

G

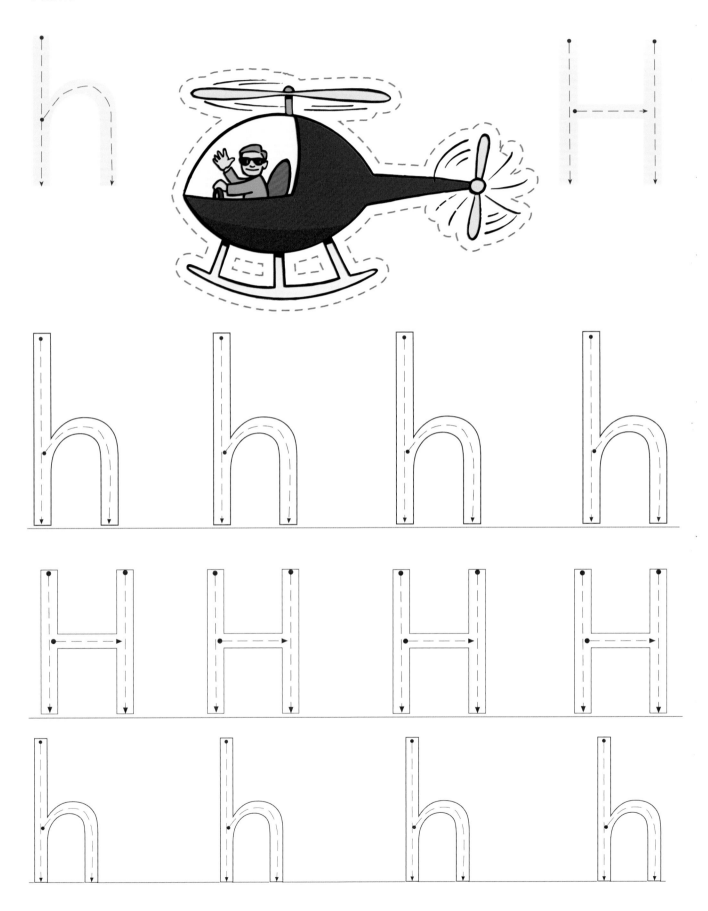

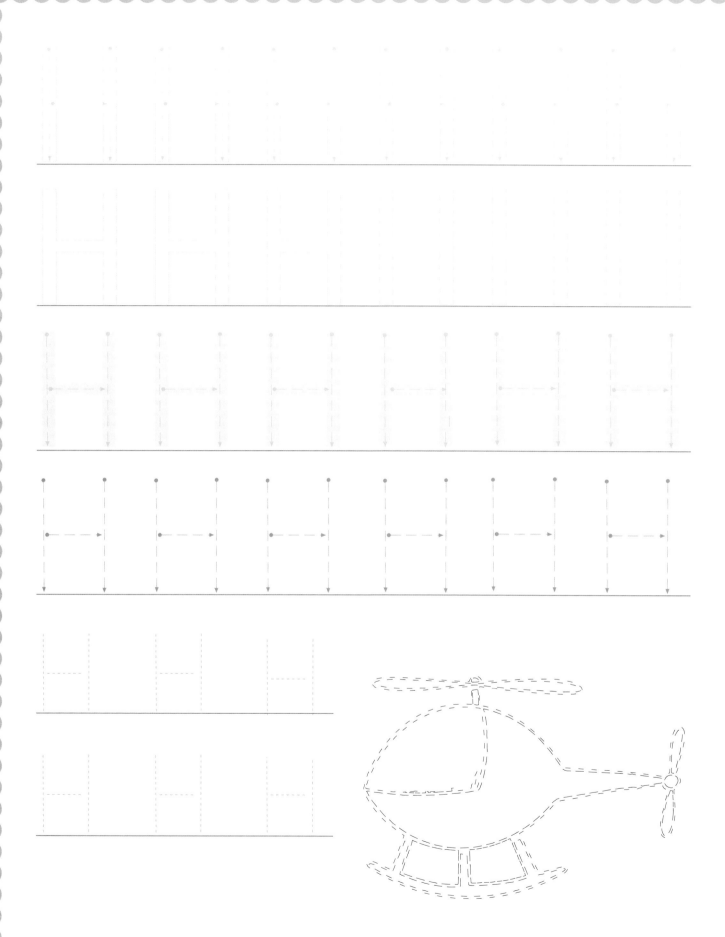

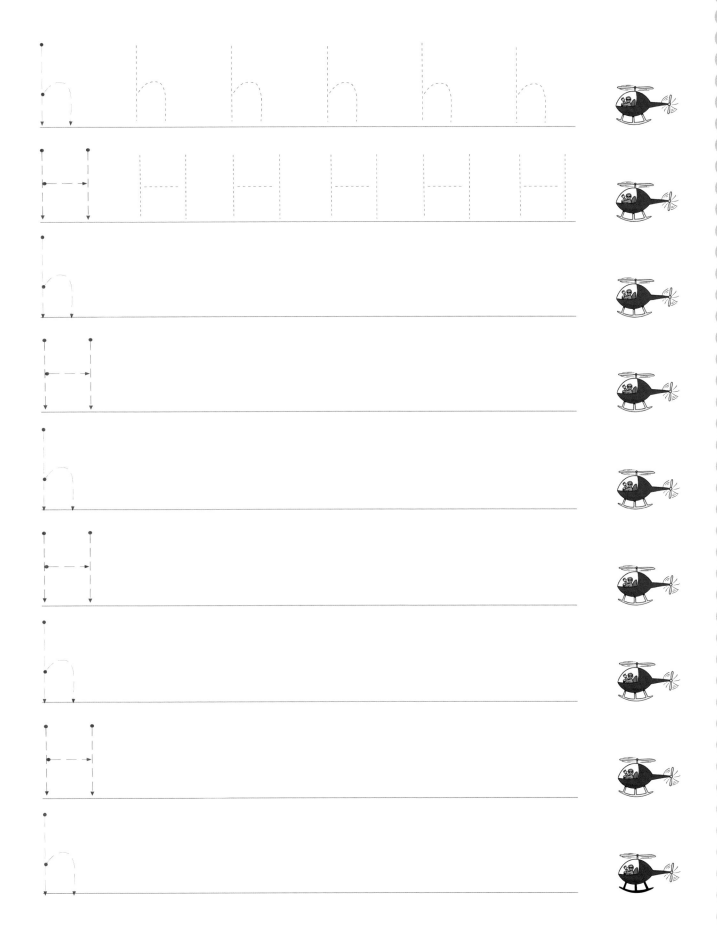

Name _____

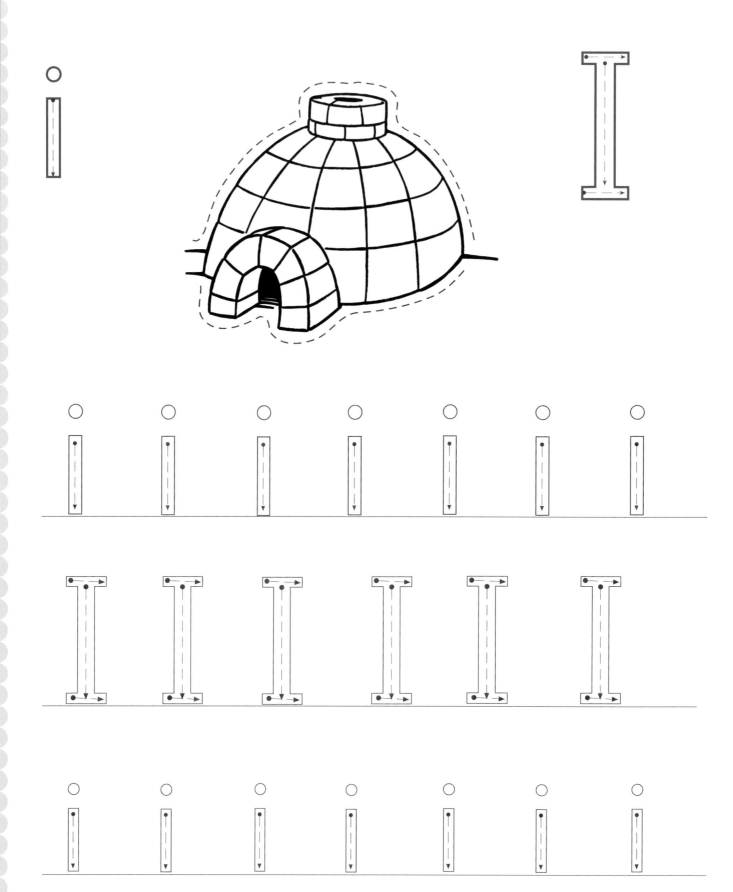

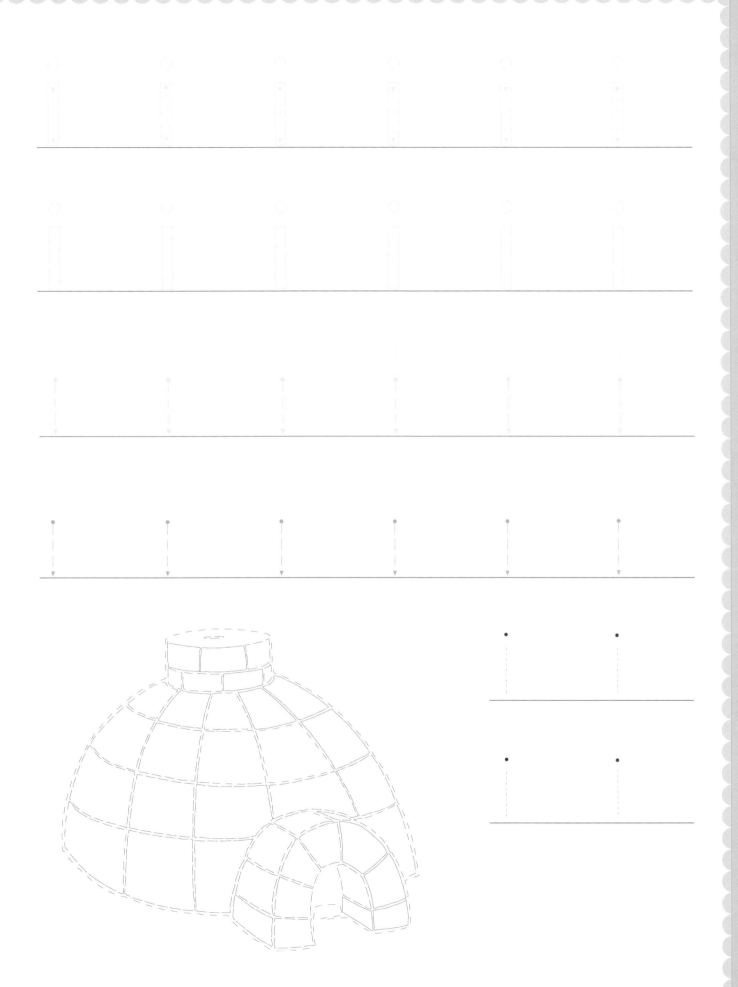

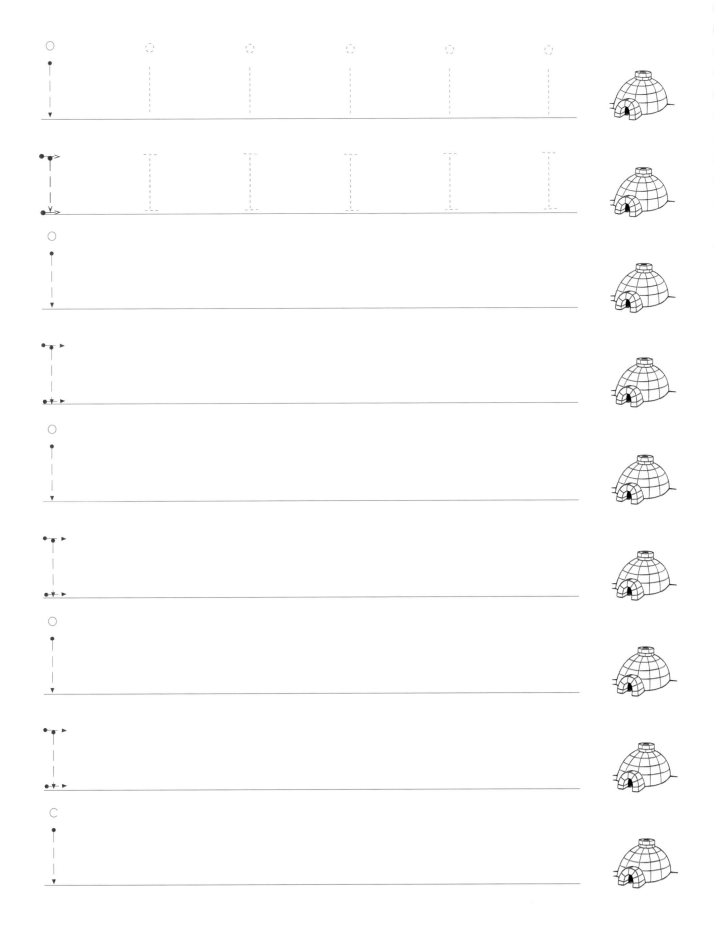

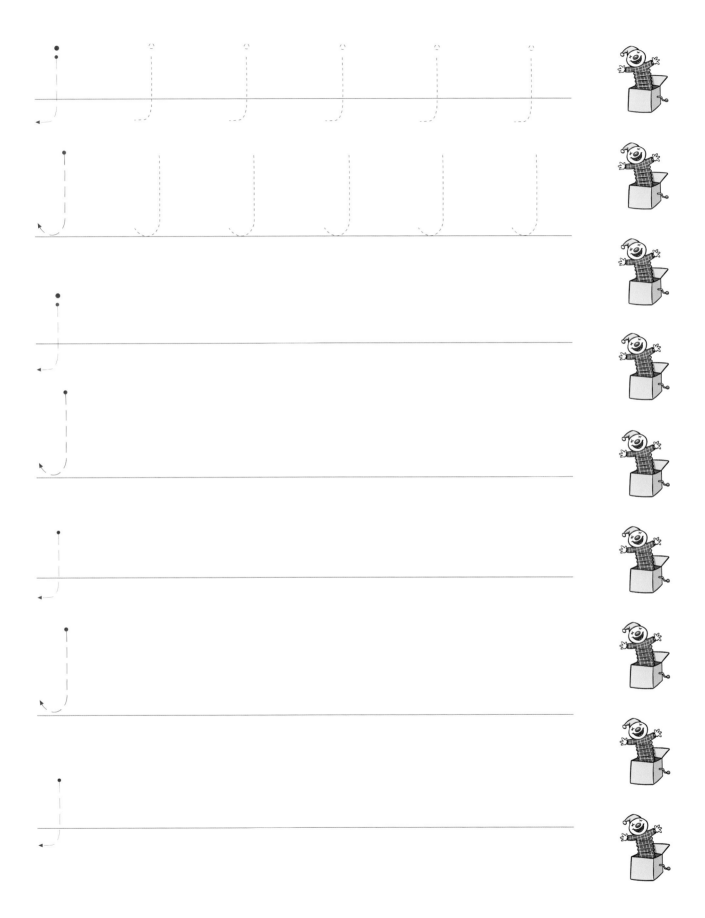

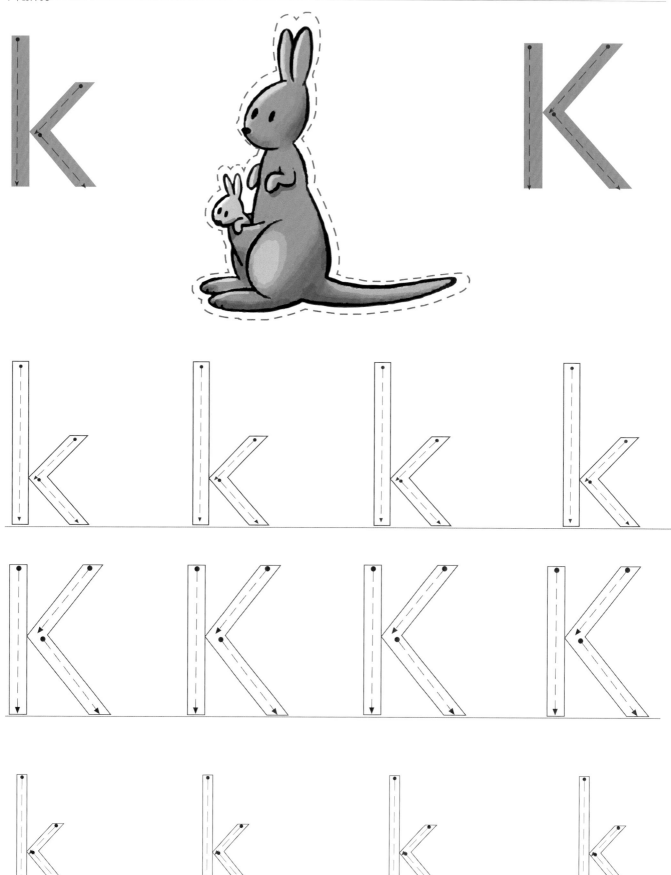

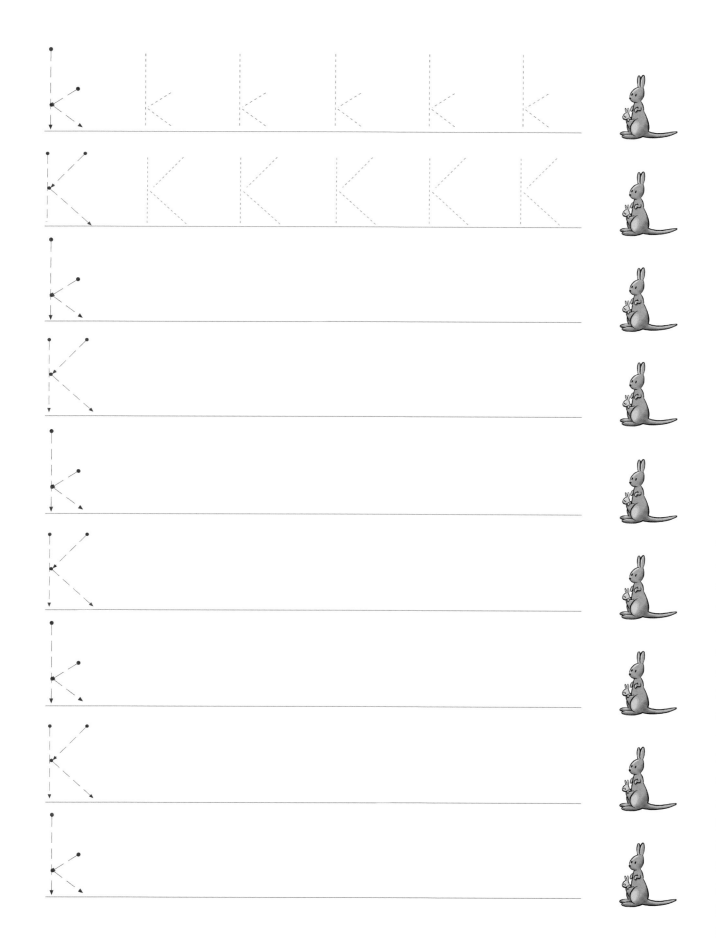

l   L

l l l l l l l

L L L L L

l l l l l l l

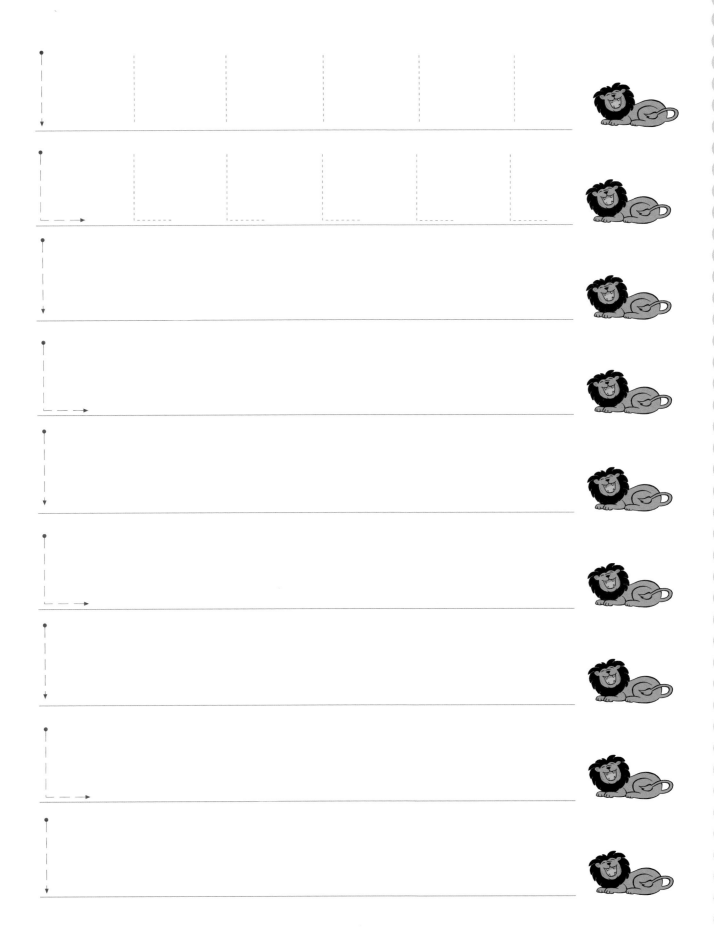

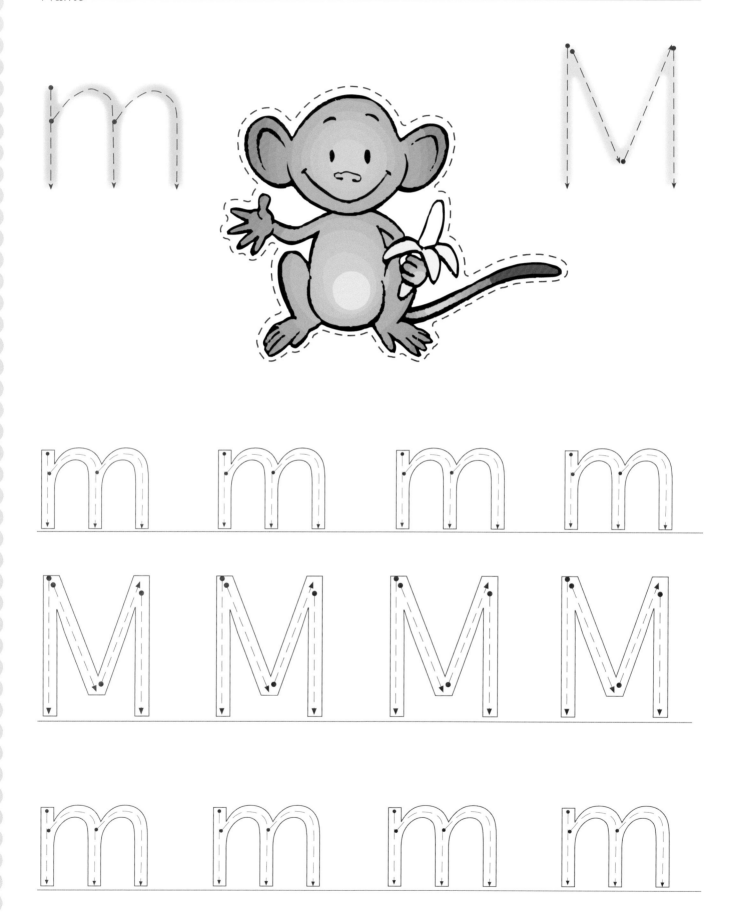

m m m m m m m m

m m m m m m m m

m m m m m m m m

m m m m m m

m m m m m m

m m m

M M M M M

M M M M M

M M M M M

M M M M M

M M M

M M M

n n n n n n

n n n n n n

n n n n n n

n n n n n n

n n n

n n n

Name _____

p · P

p p p p

P P P

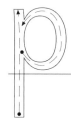  p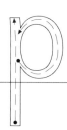

p p p p p p

p p p p p p

p p p p p p

p p p p p p

p p p

p p p

P P P P P

P P P P P P

P P P P P P

P P P

P P P

q q q q q q q q q q

q q q q q q q q q q

q q q q q q

q q q q q q

q q q

q q q

R R R R R R

R R R R

R R R R R

R R R R R R

R R R

R R R

S S

S S S S

S S S S

S S S S

S S S S S S

S S S S S

S S S S S S

S S S S S S

S S S

S S S

S S S S S S

S S S S S S

S S S S S S

S S S S S S

S S S

S S S

S S S S S S S

S S S S S S

t   T

t t t t

T T T T

t t t t

t t t t t t

t t t t t t

t t t t t t

t t t t t t

t t t

t t t

Name _____

u U

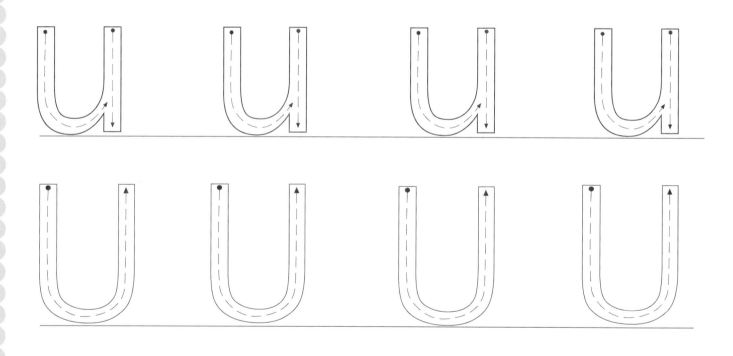

U U U U U U U U

U U U U U U U

U U U U U U U

U U U U U U U

U U U

U U U

U U U U U U

U U U U U U

U U U U U U

U U U U U U

U U U

U U U

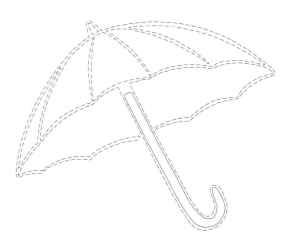

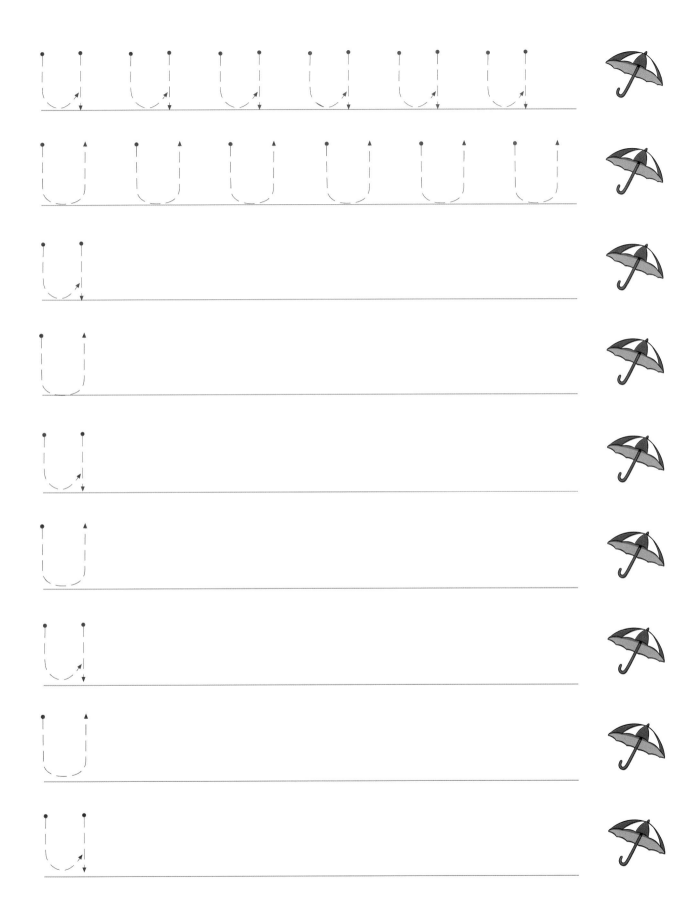

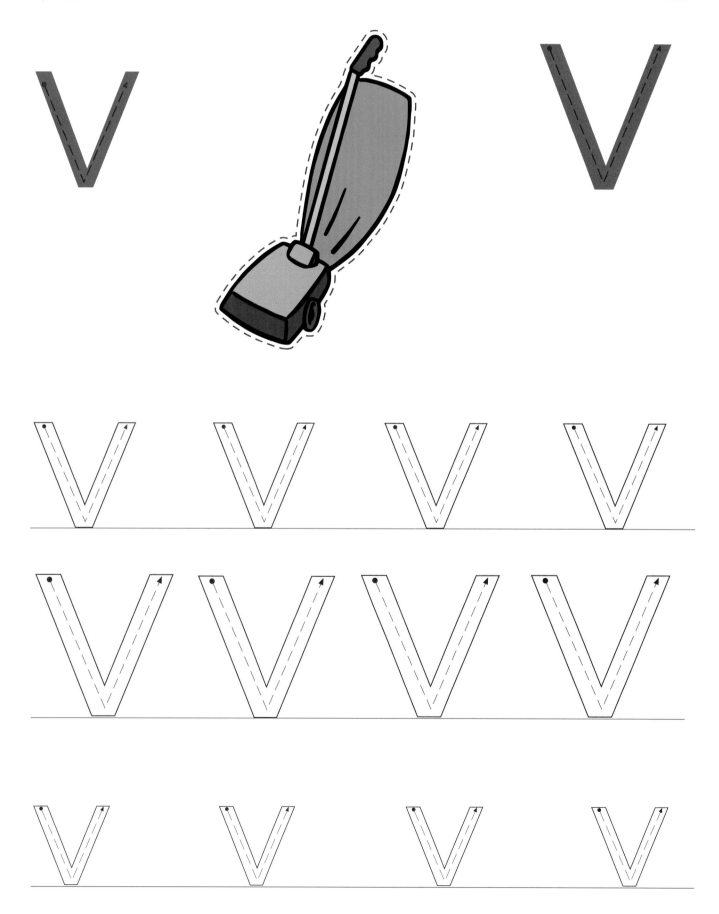

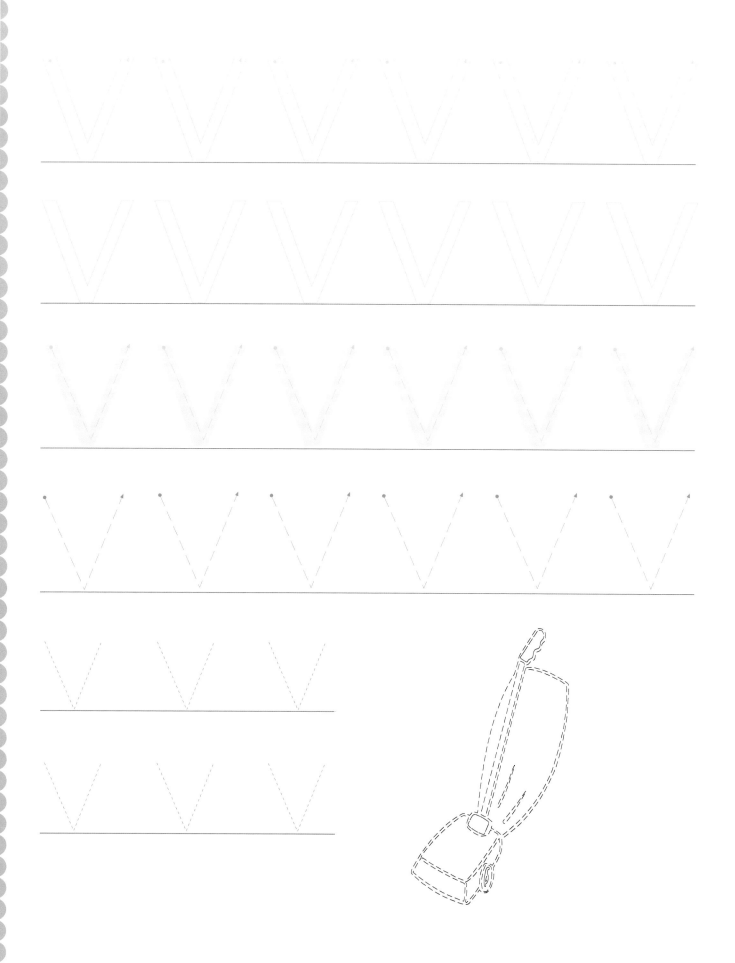

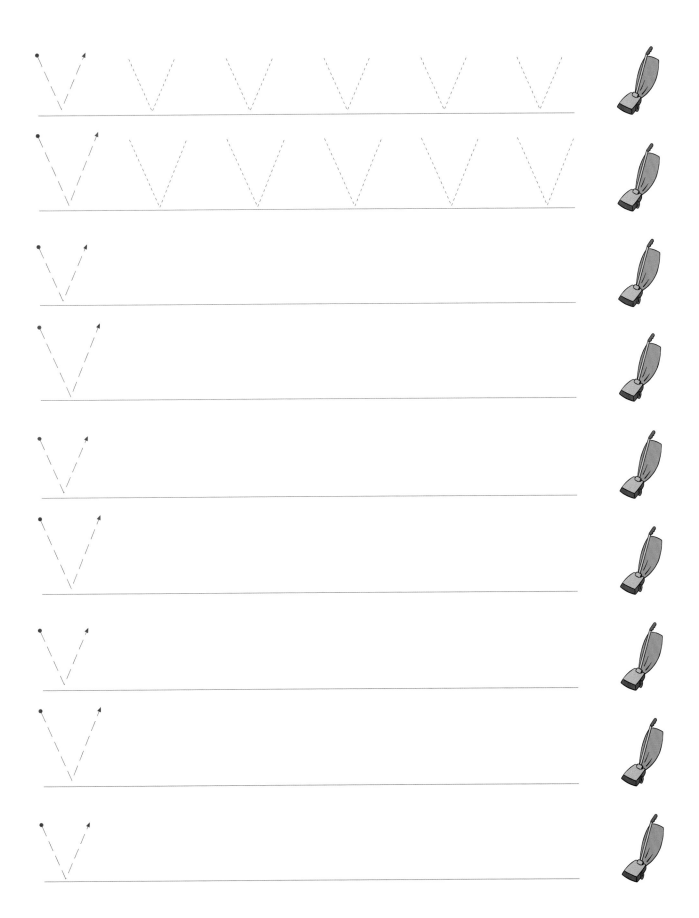

W W W W W W

W W W W W W

W W W W W W

W W W W W W

W W W

W W W

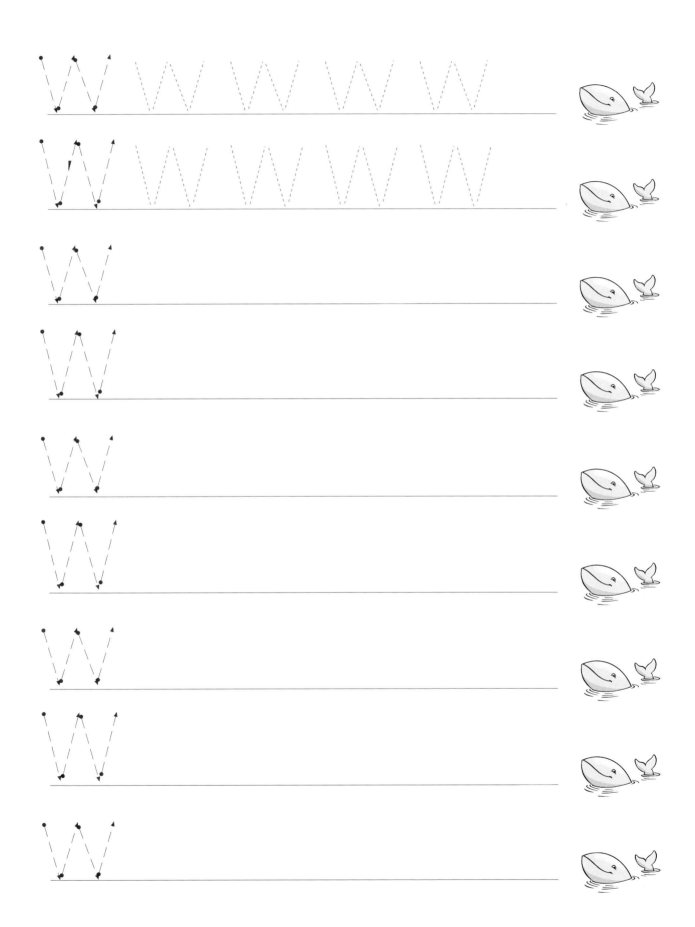

Name _____

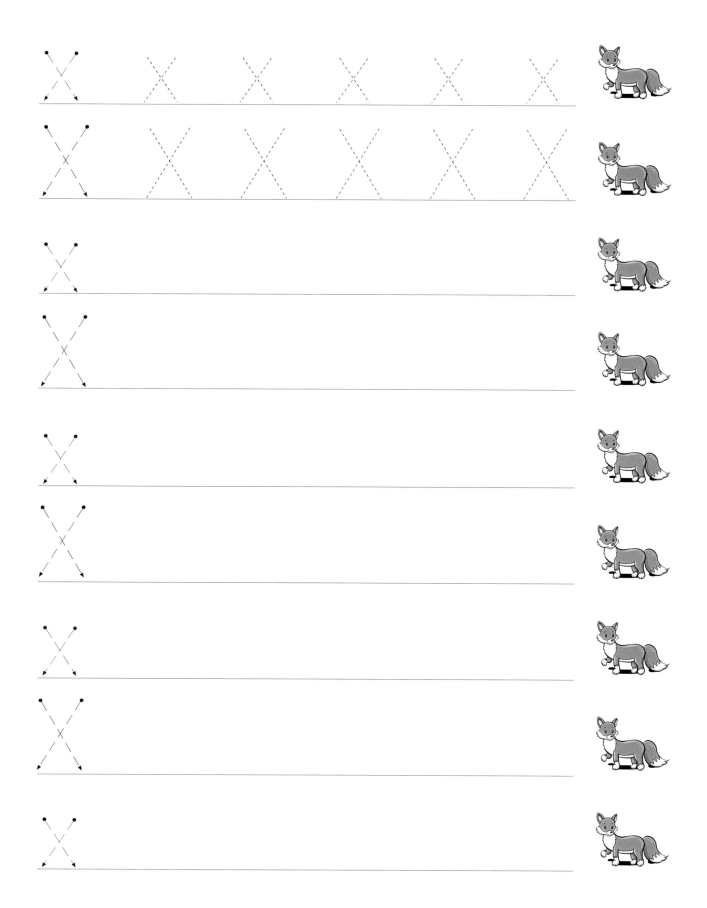

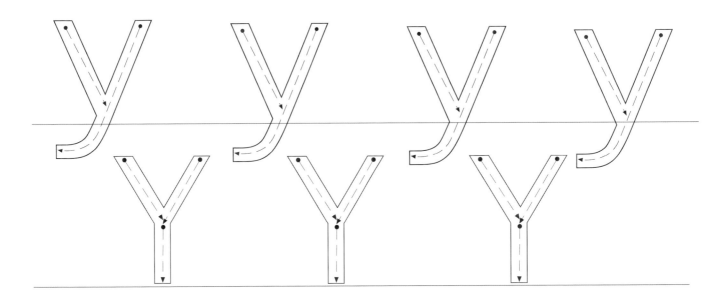

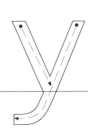
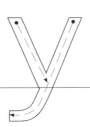
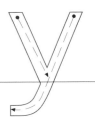

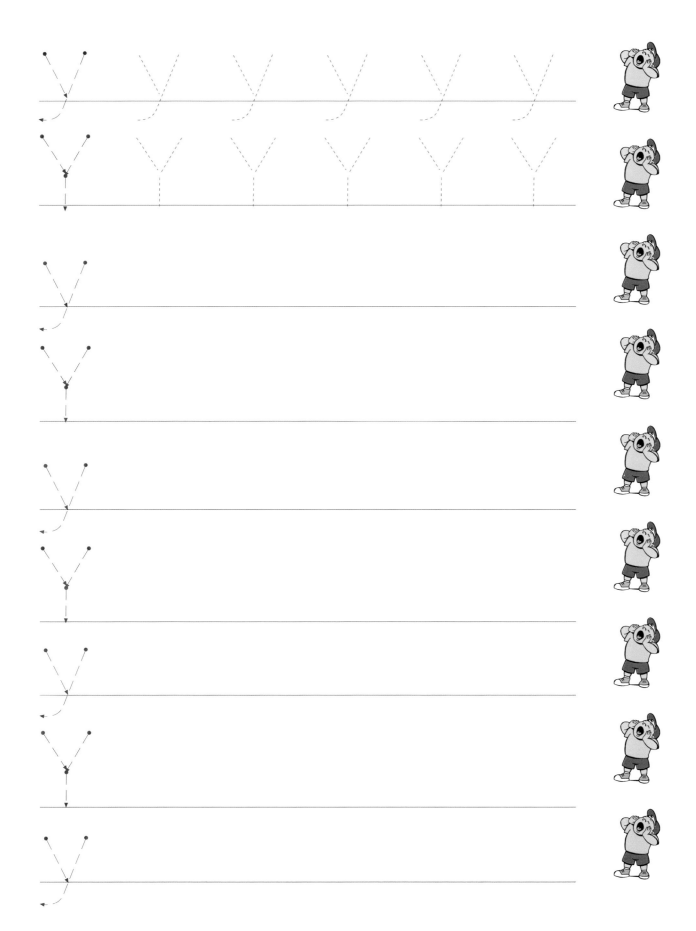

Z  Z

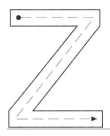 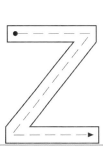 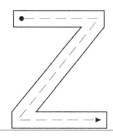 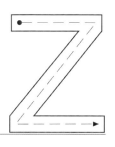

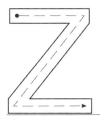   

Z Z Z Z Z Z

Z Z Z Z Z Z

Z Z Z Z Z Z

Z Z Z Z Z Z

Z Z Z

Z

2 2 2 2 2 2

2 2 2 2 2 2

2 2 2 2 2 2

2 2 2

2 2

2

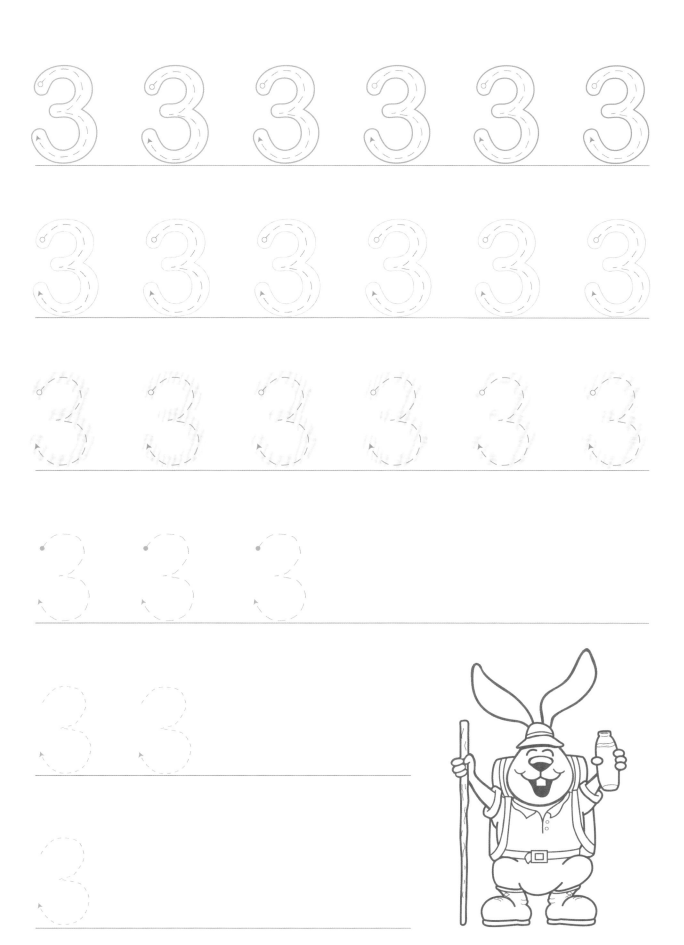

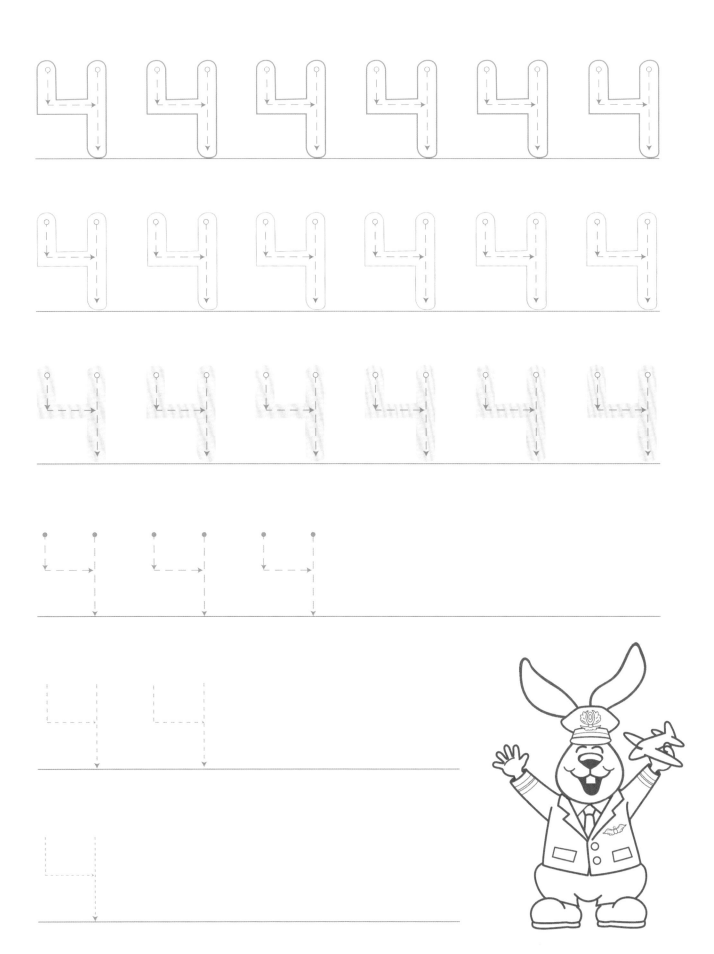

5 5 5 5 5 5

5 5 5 5 5 5

5 5 5 5 5 5

5 5 5

5 5

5

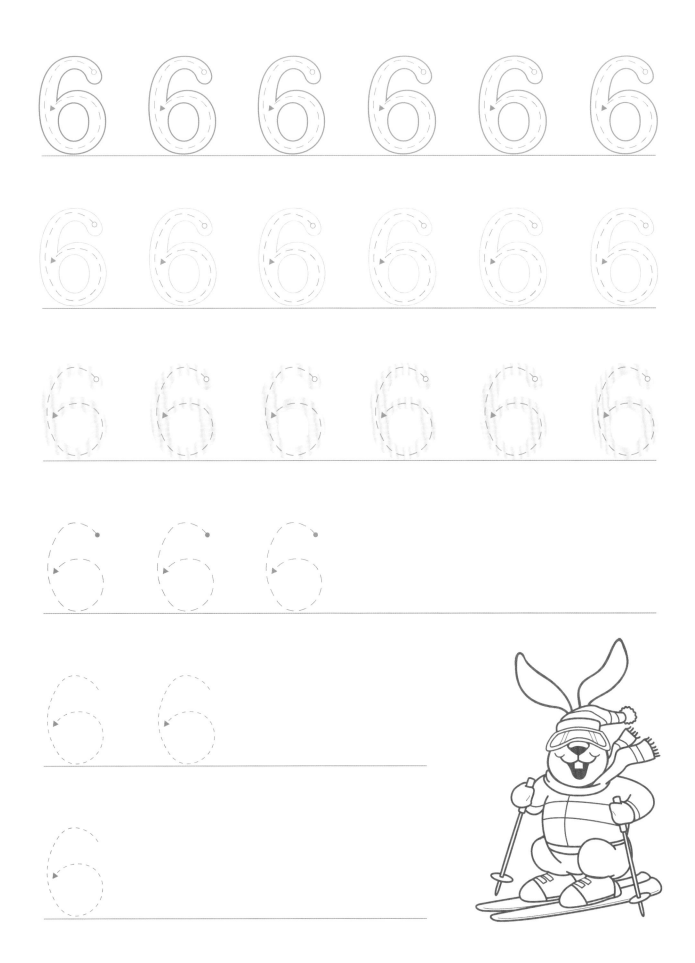

Teach your child to read with the award-winning READING LESSON. Twenty easy-to-follow step-by-step lessons will take your child from no reading skills to the second grade level.

Available at your bookstore or online; 444 pages, black and white. Color eBook is available on Kindle for your ipad and smart phone.

Find free sample lessons on our website.

WWW.READINGLESSON.COM

Giggle Bunny's
Reading Lesson software

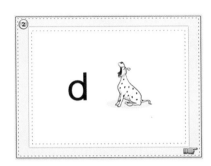

Giggle Bunny's READING LESSON companion software is an animated interactive program. An entertaining host, Giggle Bunny, will teach your child to read the fun way.

The program closely follows the READING LESSON book. With the help of lively animated characters, the letter sounds and words come alive. In every lesson, you will find Word Theater, games with trophies, and typing practice. Giggle Bunny makes it a joy.

The program is available as a download on our website.
For Windows PC only. Not compatible with iPad, iPhone or Mac.

WWW.READINGLESSON.COM

Giggle Bunny's Storybook software

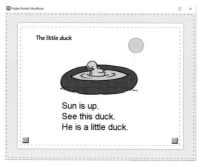

THE STORYBOOK animated program contains 40 short stories. These stories reinforce the key words learned in the READING LESSON.

The stories are simple at first and get longer and more complex as we go on. At the beginning of each story, there is a list of new words. They sound out when clicked, and phonic units are highlighted.

The animations are charming and full of surprises. The pages are clean, and the text is easy to read.

Printable version of the stories is included with the program. Your child can print out a story and make a little book out of it.

The program is available as a download from our website.

WWW.READINGLESSON.COM

Teach Me Writing book

TEACH ME WRITING naturally follows and builds on the ABC WRITING LESSON book. The child's mind forms a better memory of words when reading is followed by handwriting. Using this book together with the READING LESSON will speed up and improve both skills.

TEACH ME WRITING eBook comes with practice pages for each lesson, printable on demand. Here are just a few out of 120 pages in the book. Each lesson has key words and short sentences to practice.

The printed version of the book is available on Amazon.com. The download, in PDF format, compatible with both Mac and PCs, is available on our website.

WWW.READINGLESSON.COM

Kindy Math

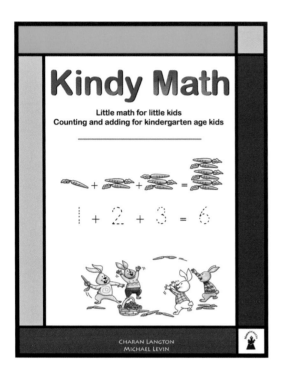

KINDY MATH book is a step-by-step primer that teaches basic math skills to your kindergartner (hence the name, Kindy Math.) Its ten lessons focus on the essential skills: counting and number order, writing numbers, and adding numbers from 1 to 10. It's a fun and easy way to introduce math to your young child.

KINDY MATH is a lead-in to the VERBAL MATH book series, which teaches math in our unique method, without paper or pencil.

After building good basic skills with Kindy Math, move on to the next step, Verbal Math Lesson 1.

Sample pages from Kindy Math book

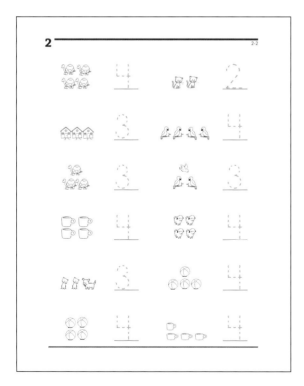

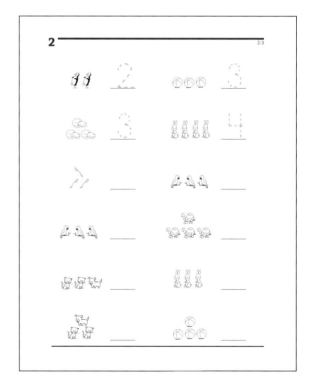

The Verbal Math Lesson series

VERBAL MATH LESSON

Step-by-step math program without pencil and paper
The BEST way to teach math to a young child!

Available on Amazon as printed books and on Kindle as
eBooks. Or order the whole eBook set from our website.

Ditch worksheets, do math the mental way.
No reading skills required.

Sample pages from the Verbal Math Lesson 1

WORKING WITH NOTHING

Let's learn the concept of 0.

Teacher: Clear a desk or a table. Place a pen and say: "There is one pen on the table." Ask: "Are there any pencils on the table?"
The answer should be: NO.

Say: "There is one pen and no pencils on the table. In math we say, there is one pen and zero pencils on the table. Zero means nothing."

EXERCISE I

Ask your child to give examples of zero. Here are some.

- If my feet are bare, that means I am wearing zero socks.
- If the road is empty, that means there are zero cars on the road.
- The garage was empty. Until my mom parked her car in it, there were zero cars in the garage.
- If no one puts money in a piggy bank, it has zero money.
- Before I planted a rose in an empty garden, there were zero roses growing there.
- After I took the last cookie from the jar, there were zero cookies left in the jar.

EXERCISE II

▶ **The rule:** *If you add a zero to a number, the number does not change.*

What is 1 + 0 = ? Child should answer: 1

2 + 0 = 2	1 + 0 = 1	0 + 2 = 2
3 + 0 = 3	0 + 1 = 1	0 + 5 = 5

What is 2 million gazillion plus zero? **Ans:** 2 million gazillion.

WORD PROBLEMS

1. We had 2 pictures on the wall and put up no new pictures. How many pictures are on the wall? **Ans:** 2 pictures
   Solution: 2 pictures + 0 pictures = 2 pictures.
   So, the answer is 2 pictures.

2. A pet store had 4 birds in a cage. No new birds were put in the cage. How many birds are in the cage now? **Ans:** 4 birds.

3. There were 10 monkeys on a tree. No new monkeys came. How many monkeys are on the tree now? **Ans:** 10 monkeys.

4. The table was empty before I put 4 plates on it. How many plates are on the table now? **Ans:** 4 plates.
   Solution: mathematically speaking, 0 plates + 4 plates = 4 plates. Therefore, the answer is 4 plates.

5. On an empty field. The construction crew built 5 houses on a field. How many houses are on the field now?
   Ans: 5 houses (0 + 5 = 5).

6. My backyard had no holes. Then 3 gophers dug 6 holes. How many holes are in my backyard now?
   Ans: 6 holes. Don't confuse holes with 3 gophers. There could have been hundreds of hole-digging gophers, but we are not counting the gophers, only the holes they dug.

7. The page was empty. Then 2 children drew 3 squares in 4 minutes. How many squares are on the page now?
   Ans: 3 squares, because (0 + 3 = 3).